BASKETBALL

Personal
Game stats

Date

Game Result

Field Goals Made

Field Goals Attemps

Field Goals %

3 PT Made

3 PT Attemps

3 PT %

Free Throws Made

Free Throws Attemps

Free Throws %

Total Points

Rebonds

Assists

Steals

Blocks

Turnovers

Fouls

Notes

Shooting Map

O For done X for fail

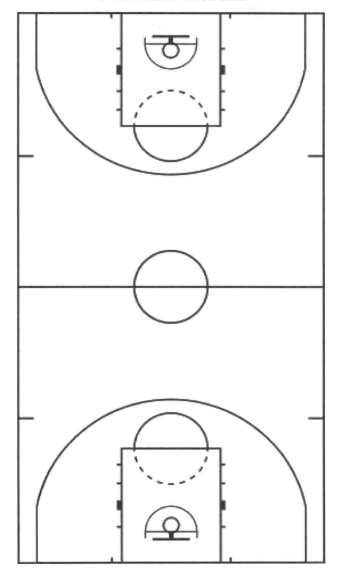

Date

Game Result

Field Goals Made

Field Goals Attemps

Field Goals %

3 PT Made

3 PT Attemps

3 PT %

Free Throws Made

Free Throws Attemps

Free Throws %

Total Points

Rebonds

Assists

Steals

Blocks

Turnovers

Fouls

Notes

Shooting Map

O For done X for fail

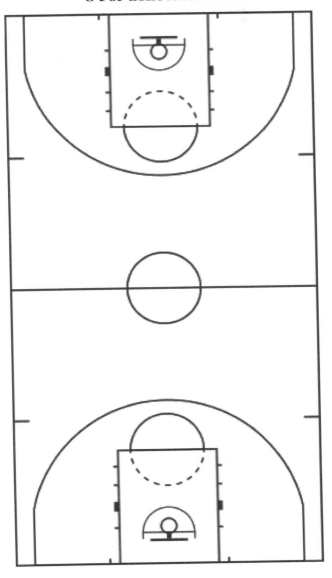

Date

Game Result

Field Goals Made

Field Goals Attemps

Field Goals %

3 PT Made

3 PT Attemps

3 PT %

Free Throws Made

Free Throws Attemps

Free Throws %

Total Points

Rebonds

Assists

Steals

Blocks

Turnovers

Fouls

Notes

Shooting Map

O For done X for fail

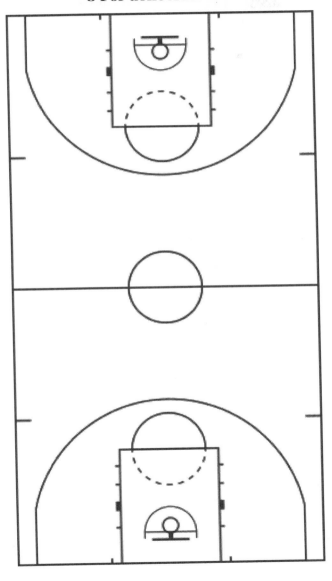

Date

Game Result

Field Goals Made

Field Goals Attemps

Field Goals %

3 PT Made

3 PT Attemps

3 PT %

Free Throws Made

Free Throws Attemps

Free Throws %

Total Points

Rebonds

Assists

Steals

Blocks

Turnovers

Fouls

Notes

Shooting Map

O For done X for fail

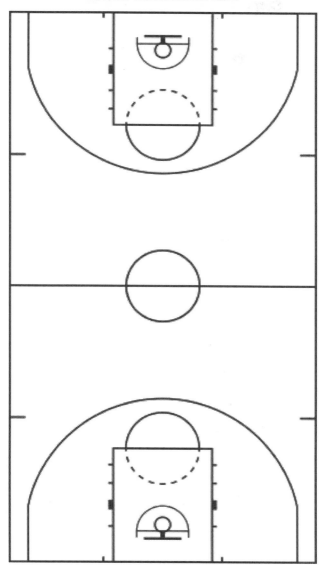

Date

Game Result

Field Goals Made

Field Goals Attemps

Field Goals %

3 PT Made

3 PT Attemps

3 PT %

Free Throws Made

Free Throws Attemps

Free Throws %

Total Points

Rebonds

Assists

Steals

Blocks

Turnovers

Fouls

Notes

Shooting Map

O For done X for fail

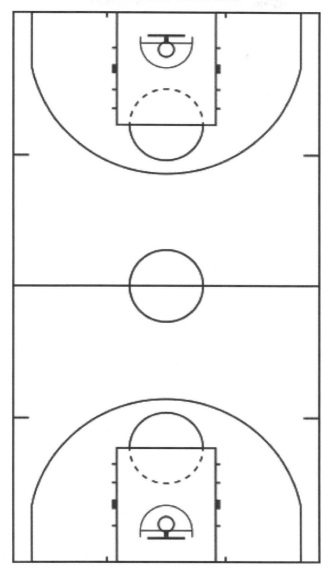

Date _____

Game Result _____

Field Goals Made _____

Field Goals Attemps _____

Field Goals % _____

3 PT Made _____

3 PT Attemps _____

3 PT % _____

Free Throws Made _____

Free Throws Attemps _____

Free Throws % _____

Total Points _____

Rebonds _____

Assists _____

Steals _____

Blocks _____

Turnovers _____

Fouls _____

Notes _____

_____

_____

_____

_____

Shooting Map

O For done X for fail

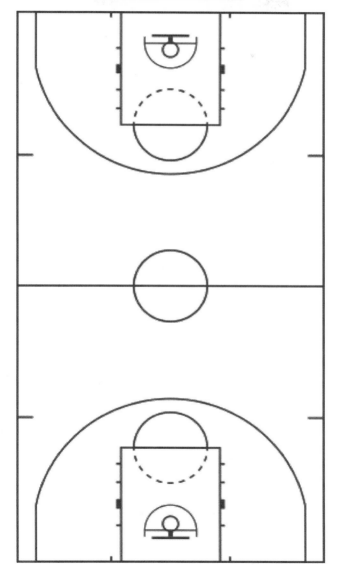

Date

Game Result

Field Goals Made

Field Goals Attemps

Field Goals %

3 PT Made

3 PT Attemps

3 PT %

Free Throws Made

Free Throws Attemps

Free Throws %

Total Points

Rebonds

Assists

Steals

Blocks

Turnovers

Fouls

Notes

Shooting Map

O For done X for fail

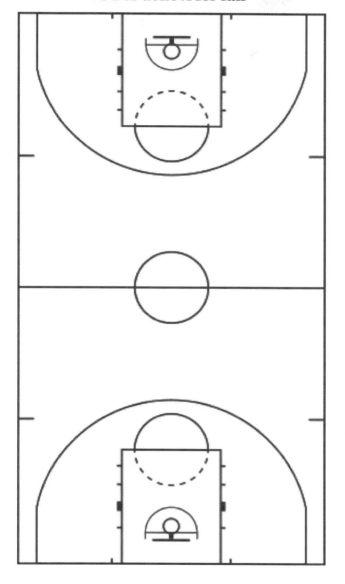

Date

Game Result

Field Goals Made

Field Goals Attemps

Field Goals %

3 PT Made

3 PT Attemps

3 PT %

Free Throws Made

Free Throws Attemps

Free Throws %

Total Points

Rebonds

Assists

Steals

Blocks

Turnovers

Fouls

Notes

Shooting Map

O For done X for fail

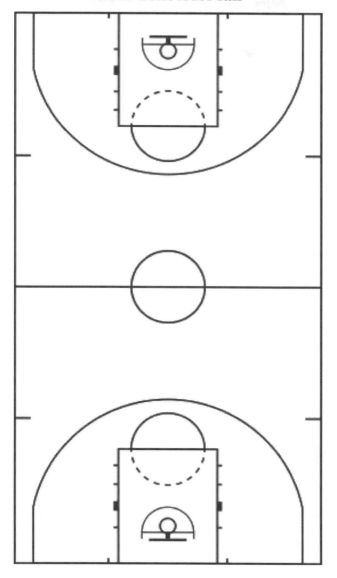

Date _____

Game Result _____

Field Goals Made _____

Field Goals Attemps _____

Field Goals % _____

3 PT Made _____

3 PT Attemps _____

3 PT % _____

Free Throws Made _____

Free Throws Attemps _____

Free Throws % _____

Total Points _____

Rebonds _____

Assists _____

Steals _____

Blocks _____

Turnovers _____

Fouls _____

Notes _____

_____

_____

_____

_____

Shooting Map

O For done X for fail

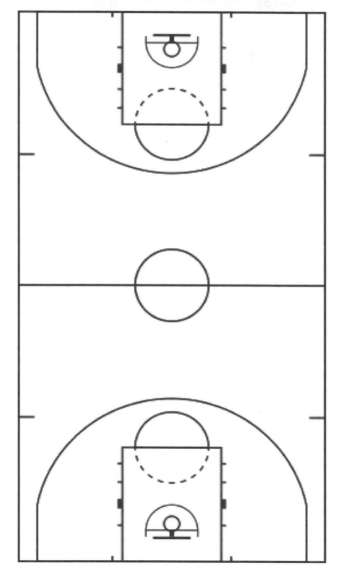

Date _____

Game Result _____

Field Goals Made _____

Field Goals Attemps _____

Field Goals % _____

3 PT Made _____

3 PT Attemps _____

3 PT % _____

Free Throws Made _____

Free Throws Attemps _____

Free Throws % _____

Total Points _____

Rebonds _____

Assists _____

Steals _____

Blocks _____

Turnovers _____

Fouls _____

Notes _____

_____

_____

_____

_____

Shooting Map

O For done X for fail

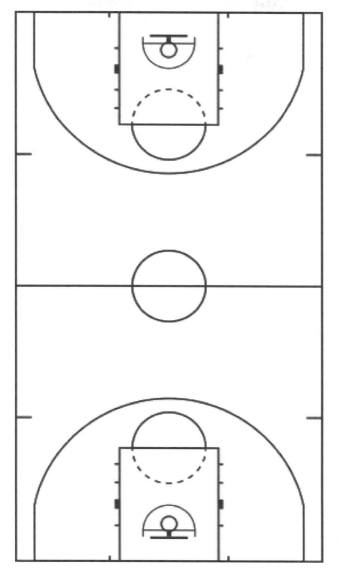

Date

Game Result

Field Goals Made

Field Goals Attemps

Field Goals %

3 PT Made

3 PT Attemps

3 PT %

Free Throws Made

Free Throws Attemps

Free Throws %

Total Points

Rebonds

Assists

Steals

Blocks

Turnovers

Fouls

Notes

Shooting Map

O For done X for fail

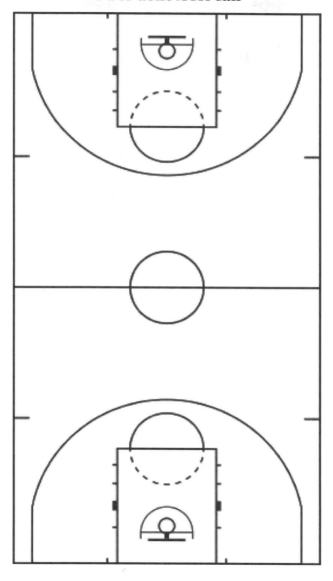

Date _____

Game Result _____

Field Goals Made _____

Field Goals Attemps _____

Field Goals % _____

3 PT Made _____

3 PT Attemps _____

3 PT % _____

Free Throws Made _____

Free Throws Attemps _____

Free Throws % _____

Total Points _____

Rebonds _____

Assists _____

Steals _____

Blocks _____

Turnovers _____

Fouls _____

Notes _____

_____

_____

_____

_____

Shooting Map

O For done X for fail

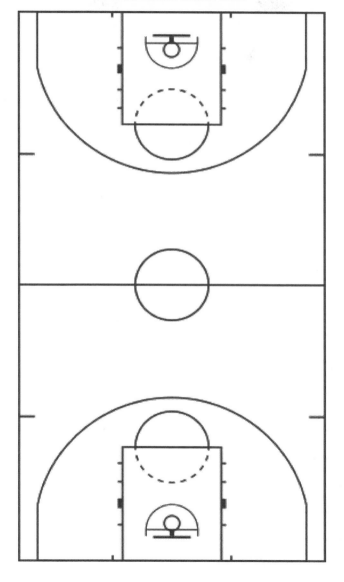

Date

Game Result

Field Goals Made

Field Goals Attemps

Field Goals %

3 PT Made

3 PT Attemps

3 PT %

Free Throws Made

Free Throws Attemps

Free Throws %

Total Points

Rebonds

Assists

Steals

Blocks

Turnovers

Fouls

Notes

Shooting Map

O For done X for fail

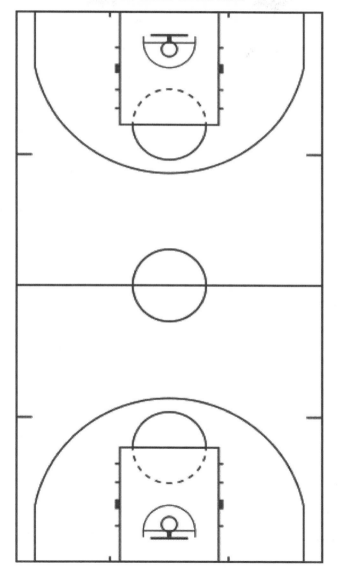

Date

Game Result

Field Goals Made

Field Goals Attemps

Field Goals %

3 PT Made

3 PT Attemps

3 PT %

Free Throws Made

Free Throws Attemps

Free Throws %

Total Points

Rebonds

Assists

Steals

Blocks

Turnovers

Fouls

Notes

Shooting Map

O For done X for fail

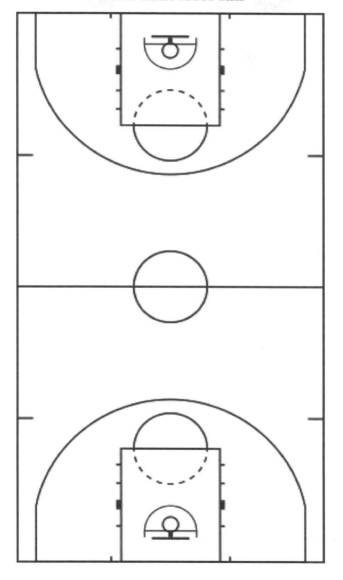

Date

Game Result

Field Goals Made

Field Goals Attemps

Field Goals %

3 PT Made

3 PT Attemps

3 PT %

Free Throws Made

Free Throws Attemps

Free Throws %

Total Points

Rebonds

Assists

Steals

Blocks

Turnovers

Fouls

Notes

Shooting Map

O For done X for fail

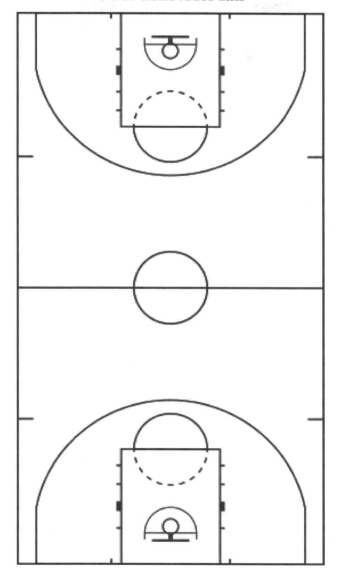

Date

Game Result

Field Goals Made

Field Goals Attemps

Field Goals %

3 PT Made

3 PT Attemps

3 PT %

Free Throws Made

Free Throws Attemps

Free Throws %

Total Points

Rebonds

Assists

Steals

Blocks

Turnovers

Fouls

Notes

Shooting Map

O For done X for fail

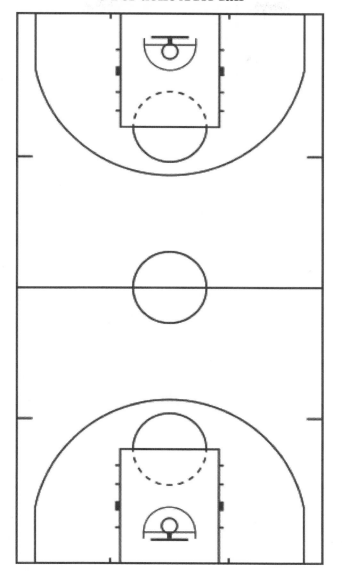

Date

Game Result

Field Goals Made

Field Goals Attemps

Field Goals %

3 PT Made

3 PT Attemps

3 PT %

Free Throws Made

Free Throws Attemps

Free Throws %

Total Points

Rebonds

Assists

Steals

Blocks

Turnovers

Fouls

Notes

Shooting Map

O For done X for fail

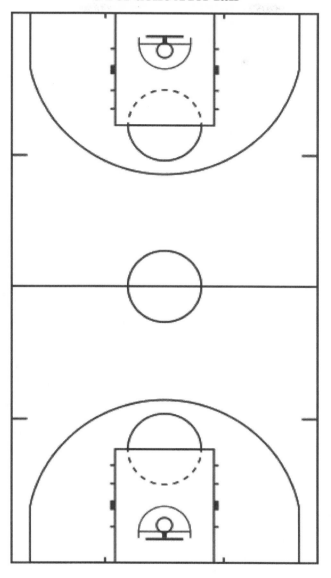

Date _____

Game Result _____

Field Goals Made _____

Field Goals Attemps _____

Field Goals % _____

3 PT Made _____

3 PT Attemps _____

3 PT % _____

Free Throws Made _____

Free Throws Attemps _____

Free Throws % _____

Total Points _____

Rebonds _____

Assists _____

Steals _____

Blocks _____

Turnovers _____

Fouls _____

Notes _____

_____

_____

_____

_____

Shooting Map

O For done X for fail

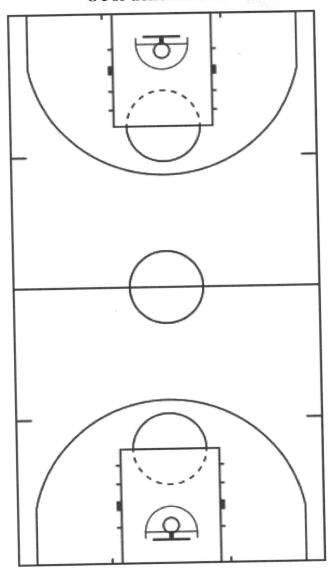

Date

Game Result

Field Goals Made

Field Goals Attemps

Field Goals %

3 PT Made

3 PT Attemps

3 PT %

Free Throws Made

Free Throws Attemps

Free Throws %

Total Points

Rebonds

Assists

Steals

Blocks

Turnovers

Fouls

Notes

Shooting Map

O For done X for fail

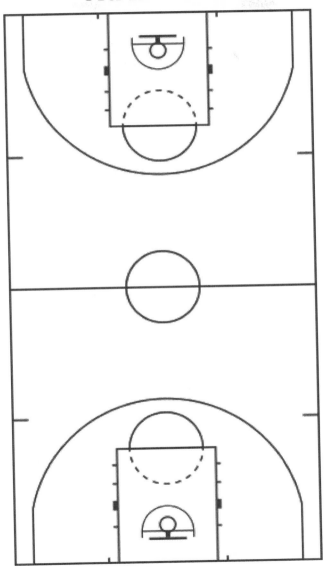

Date

Game Result

Field Goals Made

Field Goals Attemps

Field Goals %

3 PT Made

3 PT Attemps

3 PT %

Free Throws Made

Free Throws Attemps

Free Throws %

Total Points

Rebonds

Assists

Steals

Blocks

Turnovers

Fouls

Notes

Shooting Map

O For done X for fail

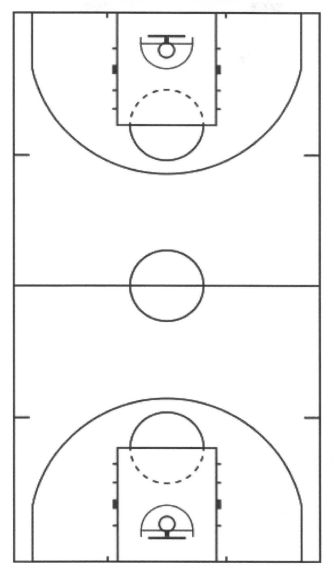

Date

Game Result

Field Goals Made

Field Goals Attemps

Field Goals %

3 PT Made

3 PT Attemps

3 PT %

Free Throws Made

Free Throws Attemps

Free Throws %

Total Points

Rebonds

Assists

Steals

Blocks

Turnovers

Fouls

Notes

Shooting Map

O For done X for fail

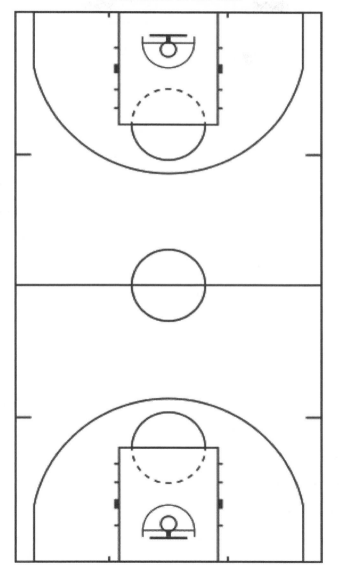

Date

Game Result

Field Goals Made

Field Goals Attemps

Field Goals %

3 PT Made

3 PT Attemps

3 PT %

Free Throws Made

Free Throws Attemps

Free Throws %

Total Points

Rebonds

Assists

Steals

Blocks

Turnovers

Fouls

Notes

Shooting Map

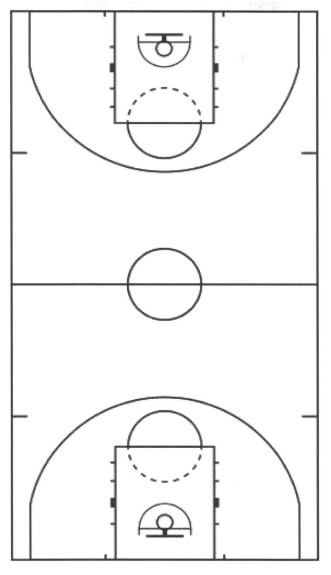

Date

Game Result

Field Goals Made

Field Goals Attemps

Field Goals %

3 PT Made

3 PT Attemps

3 PT %

Free Throws Made

Free Throws Attemps

Free Throws %

Total Points

Rebonds

Assists

Steals

Blocks

Turnovers

Fouls

Notes

Shooting Map

O For done X for fail

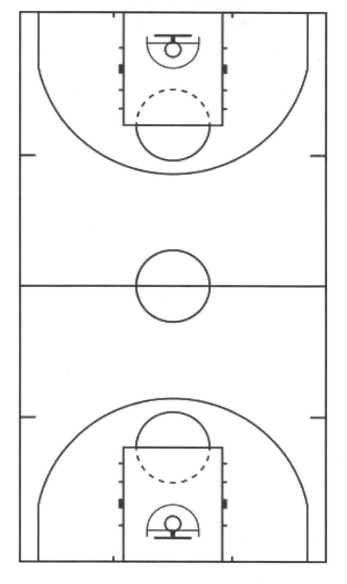

Date

Game Result

Field Goals Made

Field Goals Attemps

Field Goals %

3 PT Made

3 PT Attemps

3 PT %

Free Throws Made

Free Throws Attemps

Free Throws %

Total Points

Rebonds

Assists

Steals

Blocks

Turnovers

Fouls

Notes

Shooting Map

O For done X for fail

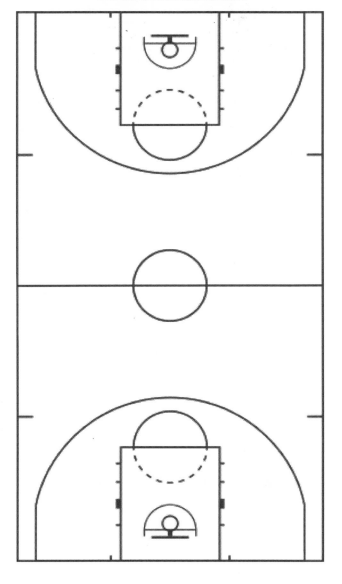

Date

Game Result

Field Goals Made

Field Goals Attemps

Field Goals %

3 PT Made

3 PT Attemps

3 PT %

Free Throws Made

Free Throws Attemps

Free Throws %

Total Points

Rebonds

Assists

Steals

Blocks

Turnovers

Fouls

Notes

Shooting Map

O For done X for fail

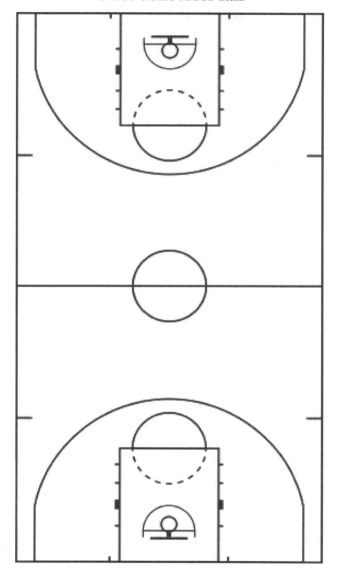

Date _____

Game Result _____

Field Goals Made _____

Field Goals Attemps _____

Field Goals % _____

3 PT Made _____

3 PT Attemps _____

3 PT % _____

Free Throws Made _____

Free Throws Attemps _____

Free Throws % _____

Total Points _____

Rebonds _____

Assists _____

Steals _____

Blocks _____

Turnovers _____

Fouls _____

Notes _____

_____

_____

_____

_____

Shooting Map

O For done X for fail

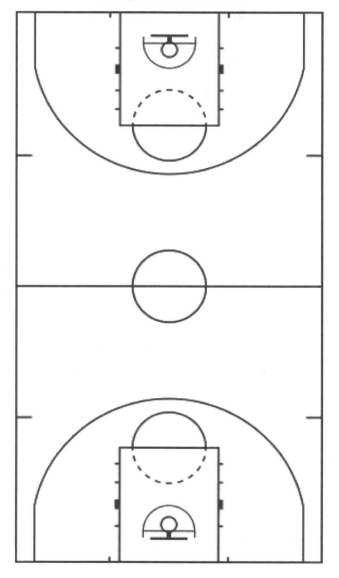

Date

Game Result

Field Goals Made

Field Goals Attemps

Field Goals %

3 PT Made

3 PT Attemps

3 PT %

Free Throws Made

Free Throws Attemps

Free Throws %

Total Points

Rebonds

Assists

Steals

Blocks

Turnovers

Fouls

Notes

Shooting Map

O For done X for fail

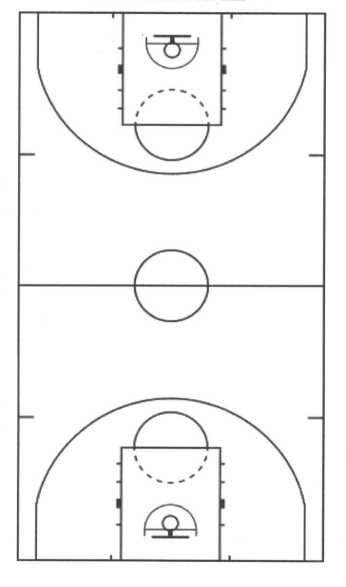

Date

Game Result

Field Goals Made

Field Goals Attemps

Field Goals %

3 PT Made

3 PT Attemps

3 PT %

Free Throws Made

Free Throws Attemps

Free Throws %

Total Points

Rebonds

Assists

Steals

Blocks

Turnovers

Fouls

Notes

Shooting Map

O For done X for fail

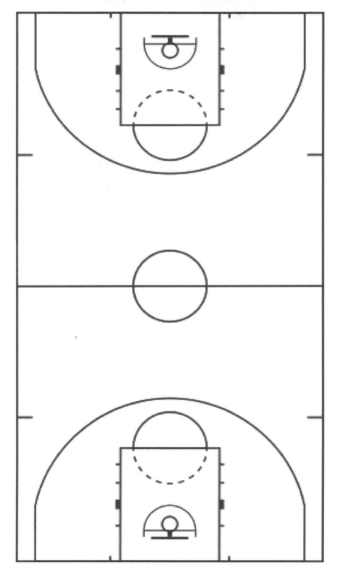

Date

Game Result

Field Goals Made

Field Goals Attemps

Field Goals %

3 PT Made

3 PT Attemps

3 PT %

Free Throws Made

Free Throws Attemps

Free Throws %

Total Points

Rebonds

Assists

Steals

Blocks

Turnovers

Fouls

Notes

Shooting Map

O For done X for fail

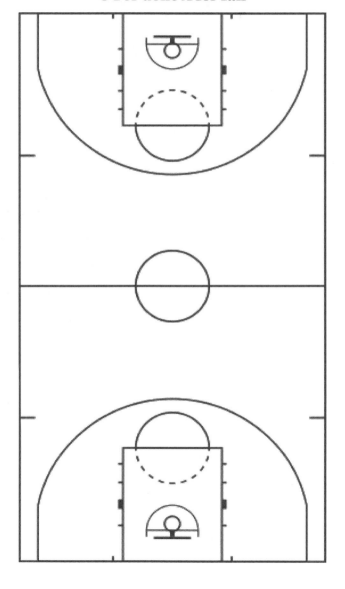

Date

Game Result

Field Goals Made

Field Goals Attemps

Field Goals %

3 PT Made

3 PT Attemps

3 PT %

Free Throws Made

Free Throws Attemps

Free Throws %

Total Points

Rebonds

Assists

Steals

Blocks

Turnovers

Fouls

Notes

Shooting Map

O For done X for fail

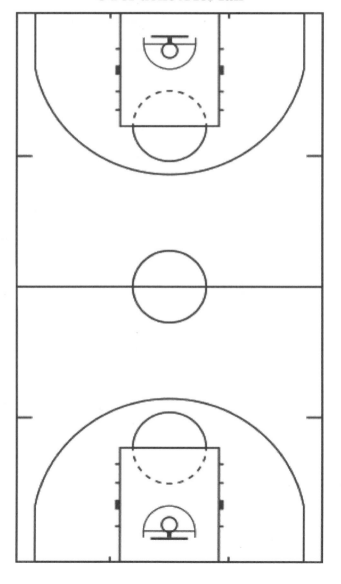

Date

Game Result

Field Goals Made

Field Goals Attemps

Field Goals %

3 PT Made

3 PT Attemps

3 PT %

Free Throws Made

Free Throws Attemps

Free Throws %

Total Points

Rebonds

Assists

Steals

Blocks

Turnovers

Fouls

Notes

Shooting Map

O For done X for fail

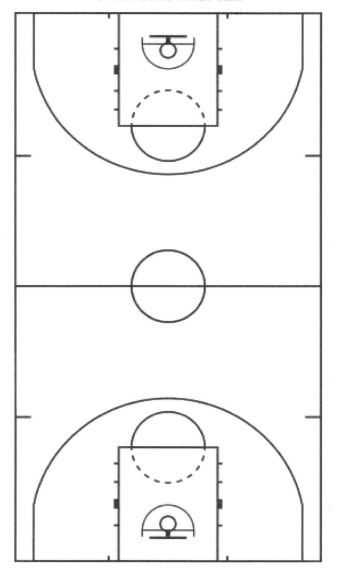

Date

Game Result

Field Goals Made

Field Goals Attemps

Field Goals %

3 PT Made

3 PT Attemps

3 PT %

Free Throws Made

Free Throws Attemps

Free Throws %

Total Points

Rebonds

Assists

Steals

Blocks

Turnovers

Fouls

Notes

Shooting Map

O For done X for fail

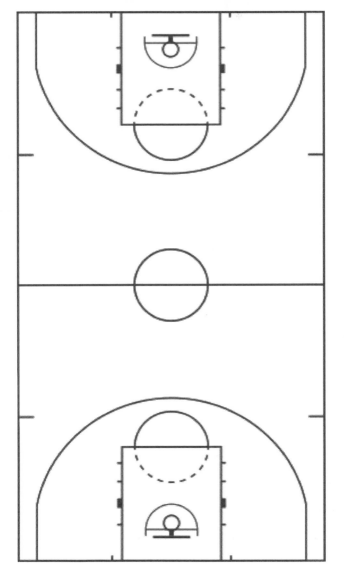

Date

Game Result

Field Goals Made

Field Goals Attemps

Field Goals %

3 PT Made

3 PT Attemps

3 PT %

Free Throws Made

Free Throws Attemps

Free Throws %

Total Points

Rebonds

Assists

Steals

Blocks

Turnovers

Fouls

Notes

Shooting Map

O For done X for fail

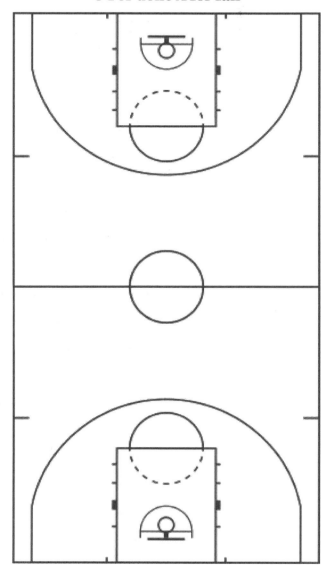

Date

Game Result

Field Goals Made

Field Goals Attemps

Field Goals %

3 PT Made

3 PT Attemps

3 PT %

Free Throws Made

Free Throws Attemps

Free Throws %

Total Points

Rebonds

Assists

Steals

Blocks

Turnovers

Fouls

Notes

Shooting Map

O For done X for fail

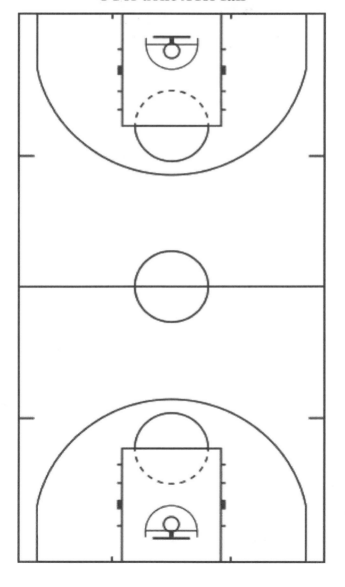

Date

Game Result

Field Goals Made

Field Goals Attemps

Field Goals %

3 PT Made

3 PT Attemps

3 PT %

Free Throws Made

Free Throws Attemps

Free Throws %

Total Points

Rebonds

Assists

Steals

Blocks

Turnovers

Fouls

Notes

Shooting Map

O For done X for fail

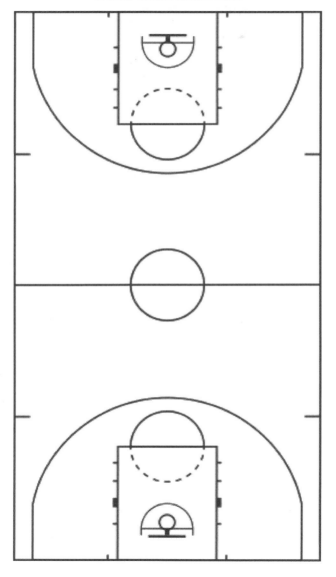

Date

Game Result

Field Goals Made

Field Goals Attemps

Field Goals %

3 PT Made

3 PT Attemps

3 PT %

Free Throws Made

Free Throws Attemps

Free Throws %

Total Points

Rebonds

Assists

Steals

Blocks

Turnovers

Fouls

Notes

Shooting Map

O For done X for fail

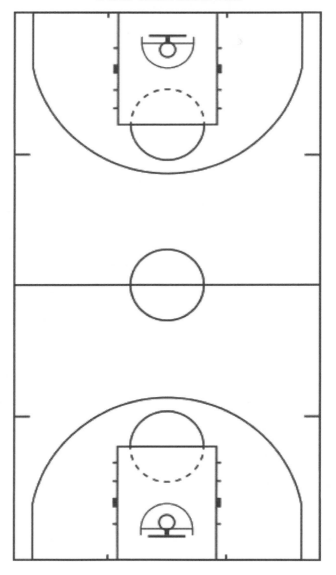

Date

Game Result

Field Goals Made

Field Goals Attemps

Field Goals %

3 PT Made

3 PT Attemps

3 PT %

Free Throws Made

Free Throws Attemps

Free Throws %

Total Points

Rebonds

Assists

Steals

Blocks

Turnovers

Fouls

Notes

Shooting Map

O For done X for fail

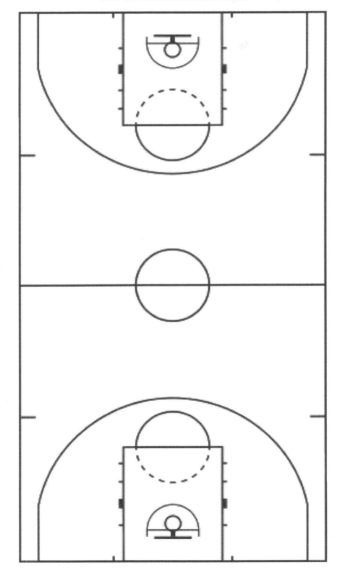

Date

Game Result

Field Goals Made

Field Goals Attemps

Field Goals %

3 PT Made

3 PT Attemps

3 PT %

Free Throws Made

Free Throws Attemps

Free Throws %

Total Points

Rebonds

Assists

Steals

Blocks

Turnovers

Fouls

Notes

Shooting Map

O For done X for fail

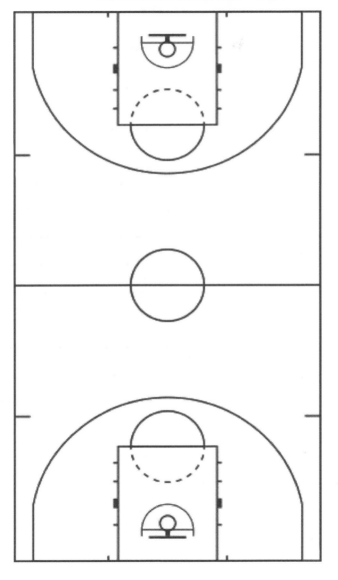

Date

Game Result

Field Goals Made

Field Goals Attemps

Field Goals %

3 PT Made

3 PT Attemps

3 PT %

Free Throws Made

Free Throws Attemps

Free Throws %

Total Points

Rebonds

Assists

Steals

Blocks

Turnovers

Fouls

Notes

Shooting Map

O For done X for fail

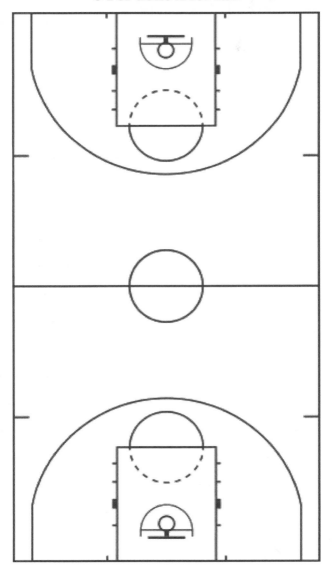

Date

Game Result

Field Goals Made

Field Goals Attemps

Field Goals %

3 PT Made

3 PT Attemps

3 PT %

Free Throws Made

Free Throws Attemps

Free Throws %

Total Points

Rebonds

Assists

Steals

Blocks

Turnovers

Fouls

Notes

Shooting Map

O For done X for fail

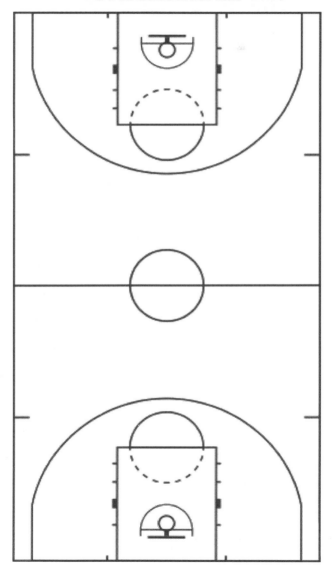

Date

Game Result

Field Goals Made

Field Goals Attemps

Field Goals %

3 PT Made

3 PT Attemps

3 PT %

Free Throws Made

Free Throws Attemps

Free Throws %

Total Points

Rebonds

Assists

Steals

Blocks

Turnovers

Fouls

Notes

Shooting Map

O For done X for fail

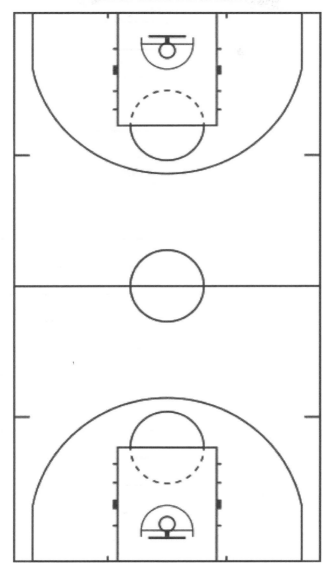

Date

Game Result

Field Goals Made

Field Goals Attemps

Field Goals %

3 PT Made

3 PT Attemps

3 PT %

Free Throws Made

Free Throws Attemps

Free Throws %

Total Points

Rebonds

Assists

Steals

Blocks

Turnovers

Fouls

Notes

Shooting Map

O For done X for fail

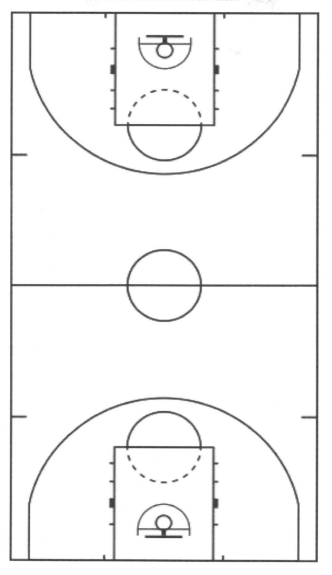

Date

Game Result

Field Goals Made

Field Goals Attemps

Field Goals %

3 PT Made

3 PT Attemps

3 PT %

Free Throws Made

Free Throws Attemps

Free Throws %

Total Points

Rebonds

Assists

Steals

Blocks

Turnovers

Fouls

Notes

Shooting Map

O For done X for fail

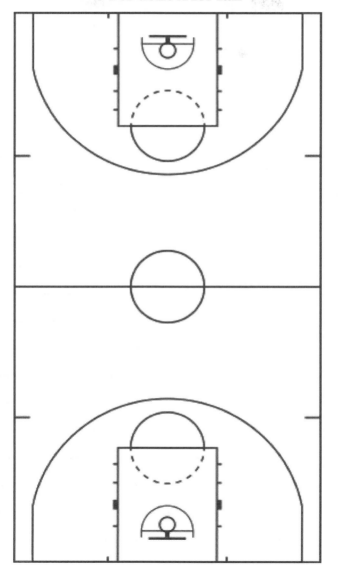

Date

Game Result

Field Goals Made

Field Goals Attemps

Field Goals %

3 PT Made

3 PT Attemps

3 PT %

Free Throws Made

Free Throws Attemps

Free Throws %

Total Points

Rebonds

Assists

Steals

Blocks

Turnovers

Fouls

Notes

Shooting Map

O For done X for fail

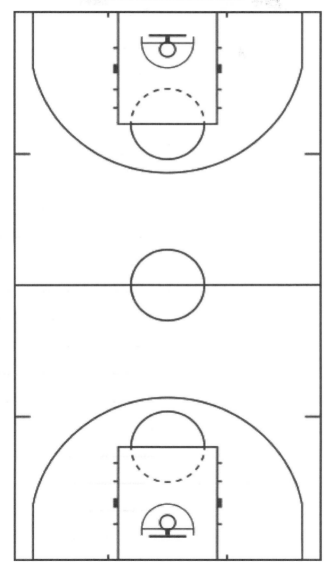

Date

Game Result

Field Goals Made

Field Goals Attemps

Field Goals %

3 PT Made

3 PT Attemps

3 PT %

Free Throws Made

Free Throws Attemps

Free Throws %

Total Points

Rebonds

Assists

Steals

Blocks

Turnovers

Fouls

Notes

Shooting Map

O For done X for fail

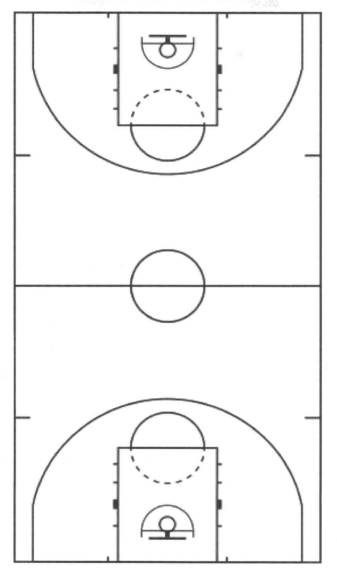

Date

Game Result

Field Goals Made

Field Goals Attemps

Field Goals %

3 PT Made

3 PT Attemps

3 PT %

Free Throws Made

Free Throws Attemps

Free Throws %

Total Points

Rebonds

Assists

Steals

Blocks

Turnovers

Fouls

Notes

Shooting Map

O For done X for fail

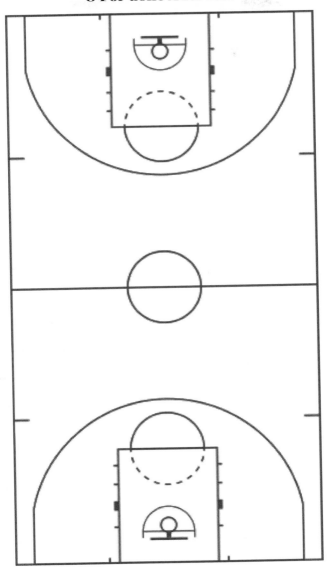

Date

Game Result

Field Goals Made

Field Goals Attemps

Field Goals %

3 PT Made

3 PT Attemps

3 PT %

Free Throws Made

Free Throws Attemps

Free Throws %

Total Points

Rebonds

Assists

Steals

Blocks

Turnovers

Fouls

Notes

Shooting Map

O For done X for fail

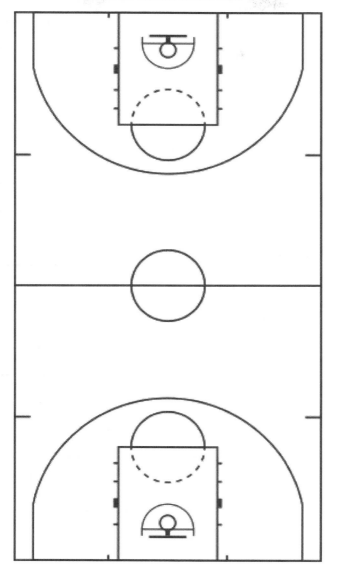

Date

Game Result

Field Goals Made

Field Goals Attemps

Field Goals %

3 PT Made

3 PT Attemps

3 PT %

Free Throws Made

Free Throws Attemps

Free Throws %

Total Points

Rebonds

Assists

Steals

Blocks

Turnovers

Fouls

Notes

Shooting Map

O For done X for fail

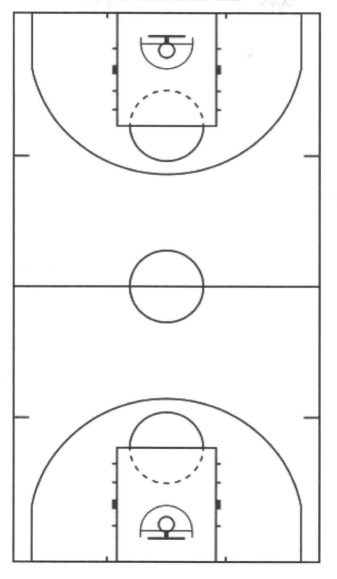

Date

Game Result

Field Goals Made

Field Goals Attemps

Field Goals %

3 PT Made

3 PT Attemps

3 PT %

Free Throws Made

Free Throws Attemps

Free Throws %

Total Points

Rebonds

Assists

Steals

Blocks

Turnovers

Fouls

Notes

Shooting Map

O For done X for fail

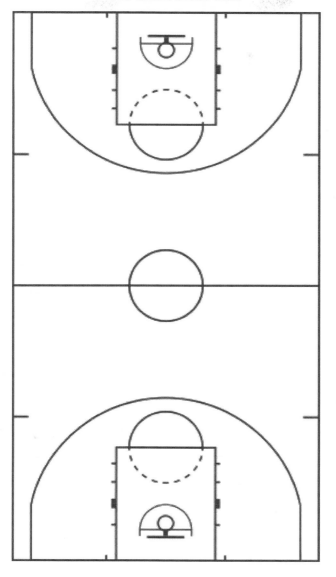

Date

Game Result

Field Goals Made

Field Goals Attemps

Field Goals %

3 PT Made

3 PT Attemps

3 PT %

Free Throws Made

Free Throws Attemps

Free Throws %

Total Points

Rebonds

Assists

Steals

Blocks

Turnovers

Fouls

Notes

Shooting Map

O For done X for fail

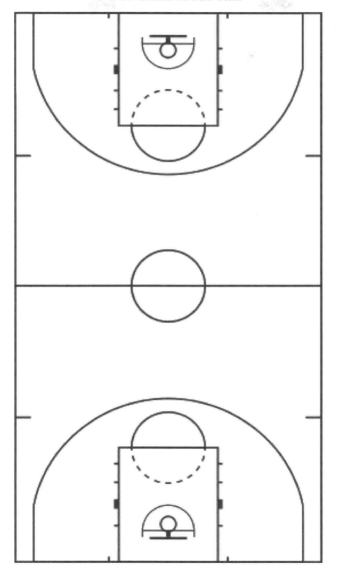

Made in the USA
Monee, IL
03 April 2023

31163195R00060